21st Century Skills Library

ANIMAL INVADERS

BULLFROG

Susan H. Gray

Cherry Lake Publishing
Ann Arbor, Michigan

Published in the United States of America by Cherry Lake Publishing
Ann Arbor, Michigan
www.cherrylakepublishing.com

Content Adviser: Randy Westbrooks, U.S. Geological Survey

Photo Credits: Cover and page 1, ©Rusty Dodson, used under license from Shutterstock, Inc.; pages 4 and 6, ©Danita Delimont/Alamy; page 9, ©E.R. Degginger/Animals Animals; pages 10 and 27, ©Grant Heilman Photography/Alamy; page 13, ©Alex Hibbert/Alamy; page 15, ©Monkey Business Images, used under license from Shutterstock, Inc.; page 16, ©David Boag/Alamy; page 18, ©Zig Leszczynski/Animals Animals; page 20, ©Chris Mattison/Alamy; page 22, ©Design Pics Inc./Alamy; page 23, ©Marvin Dembinsky Photo Associates/Alamy; page 25, ©Arco Images GmbH/Alamy

Map by XNR Productions Inc.

Library of Congress Cataloging-in-Publication Data

Gray, Susan Heinrichs.
 Bullfrog / Susan H. Gray.
   p. cm.—(Animal invaders)
 Includes index.
 ISBN-13: 978-1-60279-327-9
 ISBN-10: 1-60279-327-1
 1. Bullfrog—Juvenile fiction. I. Title. II. Series.
 QL668.E27G73 2009
 597.8'92—dc22   2008032887

Cherry Lake Publishing would like to acknowledge the work of
The Partnership for 21st Century Skills.
Please visit www.21stcenturyskills.org for more information.

TABLE OF CONTENTS

A Bullfrog Bully

Bullfrogs live near ponds and other bodies of water.

The weather is finally warming up. Bullfrogs (*Rana catesbeiana*) are becoming more active around a local pond. Two large males find a spot on the shore and begin to croak loudly—deep, rumbling croaks meant to attract females. One male stops croaking and turns to look at the other male. Then he moves closer, rises up, and gives him a shove. The other male frog tumbles sideways and into the pond. He'll find another spot soon—a spot where he can croak all night with no interruptions.

Bullfrogs are members of a large group of animals called amphibians. Frogs, toads, and salamanders are all amphibians. Most amphibians spend the early part of their lives in water, using gills to breathe. Then they develop lungs, start breathing the air, and move to land. Some amphibians, such as the bullfrog, never move completely away from the water.

21st Century Content

In many parts of the world, bullfrogs are said to be an invasive species. What exactly is that? A species is a group of the same kind of animals. For example, bullfrogs and green tree frogs are two different species of frog. Something that is invasive has moved into a new area and has taken over. The Global Invasive Species Database is a source of information on bullfrogs and many other animal invaders. People from around the world can visit *www.issg.org/ database/welcome/* to start learning more about invasive species and what is being done to control them.

CHAPTER TWO

A BULLFROG'S LIFE

A bullfrog's long legs stretch out as it jumps.

Bullfrogs are the largest frogs in North America. An adult can measure up to 8 inches (20 centimeters) from nose to rump. When leaping, the frog stretches to its full length. From the snout to the tip of the toes, it stretches out to 18 inches (46 cm). Bullfrogs weigh as much as 1.5 pounds (0.68 kilograms) each. Females are a little larger than males.

A bullfrog's legs are long and muscular. They help the frog make leaps as long as 2 yards (1.8 meters). This is more than 10 times the bullfrog's length! The toes are long and joined by thin webs of skin. Webbed feet help make the frog a good swimmer.

The bullfrog's back is light, medium, or dark green. It may be mottled or have dark brown blotches or spots. The frog's belly is usually a cream or yellow color. Its body is soft and its skin is moist.

The eyes stick up from a bullfrog's head. This allows the frog to hide just beneath the surface of a pond, with only its eyes above water. Behind each eye is a large, round eardrum. The mouth is also large. This allows the frog to grab and eat surprisingly big prey.

A bullfrog never wanders far from water. It prefers the standing water of ponds and lakes over the running water of streams. Pools that never dry up and that have plenty of plants around are the best.

As the weather warms up each year, adult males begin calling for mates. They stake out territories along the shore, sometimes wrestling each other for space. As the sun sets, they begin calling. They join together in a chorus of deep *brr-rum* sounds. Their call is a loud bellow that carries a long distance. It gives the impression that the frog is very large, which is an advantage in keeping predators away. Females are attracted to the singing, and mating soon begins.

Females lay up to 20,000 eggs in a sheet that floats on the water's surface. After a day or two, the sheet sinks out of sight. About 4 days later, the eggs begin to hatch.

Young bullfrogs look nothing like their parents. Their bodies are tiny and round. They are very dark green

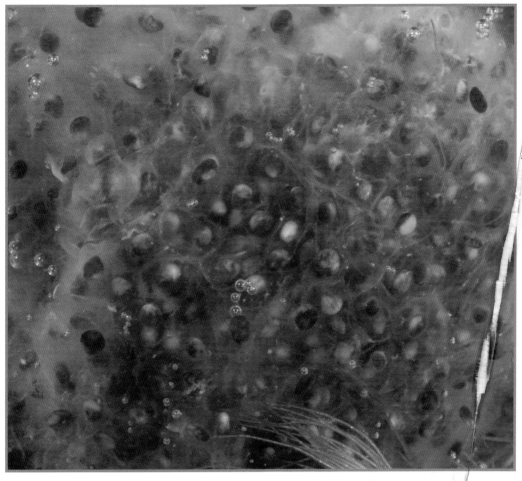

*Female bullfrogs lay eggs in a mass. The mass floats for
1 or 2 days and then sinks under the water's surface.*

or black in color. They have no legs at all, and swim by wiggling their long tails. At this young stage, they are called tadpoles. Tadpoles cannot live out of water and do not make croaking sounds. Instead, they breathe underwater

Bullfrog tadpoles don't look anything like adult bullfrogs.

by using gills. They spend their days swimming, eating, and resting. At first, tadpoles eat tiny pieces of plant material. But as they grow, they begin to eat small insects and even tadpoles of other frog species.

In time, the tadpoles' bodies begin to change. This change is called metamorphosis. As tadpoles go through metamorphosis, their tails shrink and disappear. Four little legs begin to sprout. Their snouts become pointed and their eyes bulge. Their little legs begin to kick. Lungs develop so the young frogs will soon be able to breathe air.

In warm areas, bullfrog tadpoles complete their metamorphosis in the same year they hatch. In cooler regions, they spend one or two years as tadpoles. In the winter, tadpoles find safety in the muck at the bottom of their pond. There, they hibernate, slowing their breathing and heartbeats almost to a dead stop. When warm weather returns, they become active again.

After metamorphosis, the young frogs swim using their legs. They hop around on land and breathe the air. They also develop big appetites. Like many other frogs, bullfrogs are ambush predators. A bullfrog will sit very

How does a tadpole's tail disappear? Does it just fall off? What makes it go away? These are the kinds of questions biologists asked to learn more about frog life cycles. Asking questions, observing, and experimenting led scientists to this answer.

When a tadpole loses its tail, it's because of a chemical in the tadpole's body that breaks down collagen. Collagen is a material that helps to keep tissues and cells "glued" together. When collagen breaks down in the tadpole's tail, the cells in the tail can no longer hold together. In time, materials in the cells are resorbed, or taken back into the tadpole's body, and the tail disappears completely.

still and then pounce on moving prey. Bullfrogs eat dragonflies, crawfish, fish, baby turtles, snakes, birds, and even other frogs. In turn, raccoons, snapping turtles, and large water birds, such as herons, feed on bullfrogs. Bullfrogs that escape all predators and other dangers can live for 8 or 9 years.

CHAPTER THREE

WHAT WENT WRONG

Bullfrogs often blend in with their surroundings. Can you see the bullfrog in this picture?

At one time, bullfrogs lived only in North America and only east of the Rocky Mountains. But in the early 1900s, the frogs began showing up in California and Colorado. How did they get there? Did they hop?

Bullfrogs arrived in the western United States in a few different ways. Some ended up there when people began raising bullfrogs in ponds in California to be able to sell the frogs' legs to restaurants. In the eastern part of the continent, people had enjoyed eating native bullfrog legs for years. Restaurant owners in the west heard that frog legs were delicious. They wanted to offer them to their customers. Bullfrogs ended up in other western U. S. states and in Asia, Europe, and South America in the same way.

In Colorado, bullfrogs may have been introduced by accident. Some scientists think that bullfrogs laid eggs in trout hatcheries elsewhere in the country. When the young fish were released into Colorado's trout streams and lakes, bullfrog tadpoles were released along with them.

Some people in western states also purchased bullfrogs as pets. The large frogs with the deep, rumbling voices

Frog legs are on the menu at many restaurants.

were unusual and fun to own. Some frog owners enjoyed watching the development of those huge tadpoles.

But after the tadpoles went through metamorphosis, they were no longer so interesting. The bullfrogs were often placed in backyard ponds where they ate everything in sight. Then some owners released their frogs into other nearby ponds. Even some of the people who had started frog farms lost interest and released their frogs.

This bullfrog tadpole has grown legs and will soon lose its tail.

That's when the trouble began. Food was plentiful in the bullfrogs' new homes. They settled in and began to mate. Females laid eggs by the thousands. Little tadpoles found safety among the weeds and algae. They ate the tadpoles of other frogs. Fish quickly learned that bullfrog tadpoles tasted terrible compared to the tadpoles of other frogs. So bullfrog tadpoles escaped predators while other tadpoles did not. As adults, bullfrogs ate almost any creature that fit into their mouths.

Bullfrogs also have some other advantages. They can tolerate higher water temperatures than most other frogs. They also have a longer breeding season, and their tadpoles have a higher rate of survival than the tadpoles of other frogs.

With few enemies, huge appetites, and some natural advantages, bullfrog numbers increased. Meanwhile, populations of other pond animals began to shrink.

Learning & Innovation Skills

An international organization called the Invasive Species Specialist Group (ISSG) keeps track of invasive species around the world. Dr. Mick Clout, a biologist at the University of Auckland in New Zealand, is the director of the ISSG. The group follows the spread of many species. It collects and shares information about how different countries are trying to control the invaders. Such information is very useful to organizations, such as the Nature Conservancy, that manage invasive species such as the bullfrog. Who else might be interested in such information? How is the ISSG helping people to deal with invasive species?

CHAPTER FOUR

WORLD TRAVELERS

Bullfrogs have large appetites and will even eat other frogs.

Over the last 100 years, bullfrogs have invaded many parts of the world. In addition to the western United States, they have been introduced into Canada, South America, Cuba, and Puerto Rico. They have also been introduced into many European countries, the Republic of Korea, and Japan.

The frog's huge appetite causes plenty of problems in these countries. When it moves into a new area, it competes with native frogs for food. Because it's such a big frog with such a huge mouth, it catches just about anything it aims for. Other frog species don't have a chance. On top of that, bullfrogs won't hesitate to eat those other frogs.

This can cause a whole series of problems. In California, bullfrogs prey on the red-legged frog. In recent years, bullfrogs and habitat destruction have caused the red-legged frog population

In some regions, other invasive species have actually helped the bullfrogs invade. In the state of Oregon, sunfish live in many lakes and ponds. These fish were brought in from other states, and are said to be invasive. Unfortunately, sunfish often feed on young dragonflies. Those same dragonflies would normally eat bullfrog tadpoles. So the sunfish are eating the bullfrogs' enemies. They are protecting the bullfrog invaders! How might this problem be solved? Should wildlife officials bring in another species to eat the sunfish? Why or why not?

Red-legged frogs are often eaten by bullfrogs. This is one factor that has helped make red-legged frogs an endangered species.

to shrink. In fact, red-legged frogs have become so rare that laws are in place to protect them. Unfortunately, the red-legged frog is also a favorite food of the San Francisco garter snake. The snake is so rare that it is in danger of becoming extinct. Therefore, the bullfrog is harming both species. While it preys on the rare red-legged frog, it is also helping to wipe out the food supply of the even rarer San Francisco garter snake.

In some countries, the bullfrogs pose another problem. They carry an organism called the chytrid fungus. The chytrid fungus does not seem to bother bullfrogs, but it causes a disease in other frogs. When fungus-carrying bullfrogs share a pond with other frogs, the disease spreads quickly. Spores of the fungus spread to other frogs, and they become sick. Their outer skin peels off. They move slowly and sit out in the open, failing to stay in protected areas. Many of them die. The sickened frogs may even hop to new ponds, taking the spores with them.

The National Wildlife Federation is an organization in the United States that works to protect wildlife. One of its programs is called Frogwatch USA. People across the country volunteer to help with this program. They use the opportunity to learn all about the frogs and toads that live in their area. Then, at certain times of the year, they visit wetlands where the amphibians live. They listen for their different calls, and write down what they hear. This information helps scientists to know where frog and toad populations are doing well, and where they are decreasing. It also helps them know whether bullfrogs have invaded an area, and if those bullfrogs are harming other species.

Bullfrogs are at home on land and in the water.

Bullfrogs, as a result, cause trouble in two ways. By eating so many other animals, they change the **environments** they invade. By carrying a fungus, they spread a disease that sickens and kills other frogs.

CHAPTER FIVE

A TOUGH PROBLEM

Once bullfrogs invade a pond, it can be hard to remove them from the area.

Experts believe that the best way to deal with an invasive species is to keep it from invading in the first place. This is certainly true for the bullfrog. Once it moves into an area, it is very difficult to eradicate unless action is taken very quickly.

For this reason, experts suggest that fish farmers build fences around their ponds and tanks. The fences should be high enough to prevent frogs from jumping or climbing over. Landowners with ponds should try draining them and keeping them dry until after egg-laying season. The fences and drained ponds should keep bullfrogs from moving in and spreading.

Once the bullfrog eggs are laid in a pond, it is difficult to remove them. The egg masses break up easily, so it is difficult to simply lift out the eggs with a net. Also, because the eggs sink after a couple of days, they might never be discovered. Many people simply ignore bullfrog eggs and tadpoles. They find it easier to remove the adults. They hunt them at night, using very bright lights. The lights blind the bullfrogs for a short time. In that brief moment, frog hunters can quickly grab or net them. They also sometimes shoot the frogs or spear them with a long-handled tool called a frog gig.

The bullfrog problem is too large to be solved by hunting alone.

In places where bullfrogs are invaders, hunting has little effect on the bullfrog population. But in some areas where the frogs are native, it has created problems. In Ontario, Canada, for example, bullfrogs seem to be disappearing.

This is a result of the loss of bullfrog habitat. Less habitat means fewer bullfrogs. Hunting is bringing bullfrog numbers down even more. In Ontario, bullfrog hunting is now against the law.

Some places have laws meant to stop the spread of bullfrogs. In Arizona and Utah, for example, it is against the law to move bullfrogs from one place to another. In Europe, it is illegal to import bullfrogs at all.

The story of the bullfrog is certainly complicated. In some parts of the world, the bullfrog is disappearing and is protected by law. In other areas, the frog is an invader and the law forbids owning it. It will require a lot of research and money to get the bullfrog situation

It will take the efforts of many people working together to stop the spread of bullfrogs.

under control. It will take far more money than people ever made selling them as pets or for food. But a lesson can be learned. People should think very carefully before introducing a species, such as the bullfrog, into a new area.

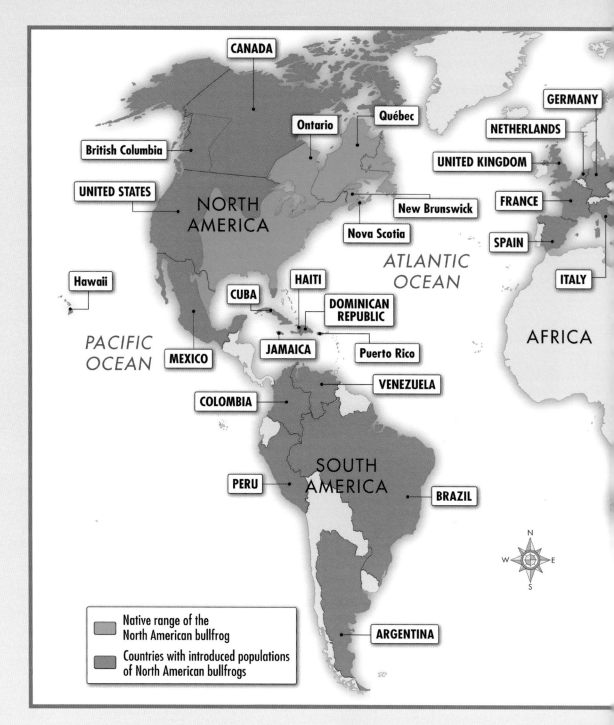

CANADA

GERMANY

Ontario

Québec

NETHERLANDS

British Columbia

UNITED KINGDOM

UNITED STATES

NORTH
AMERICA

FRANCE

New Brunswick

SPAIN

Nova Scotia

ITALY

ATLANTIC
OCEAN

Hawaii

HAITI

CUBA

DOMINICAN
REPUBLIC

AFRICA

PACIFIC
OCEAN

MEXICO

JAMAICA

Puerto Rico

VENEZUELA

COLOMBIA

SOUTH
AMERICA

PERU

BRAZIL

N

W   E

S

Native range of the
North American bullfrog

Countries with introduced populations
of North American bullfrogs

ARGENTINA

This map shows where in the world the bullfrog

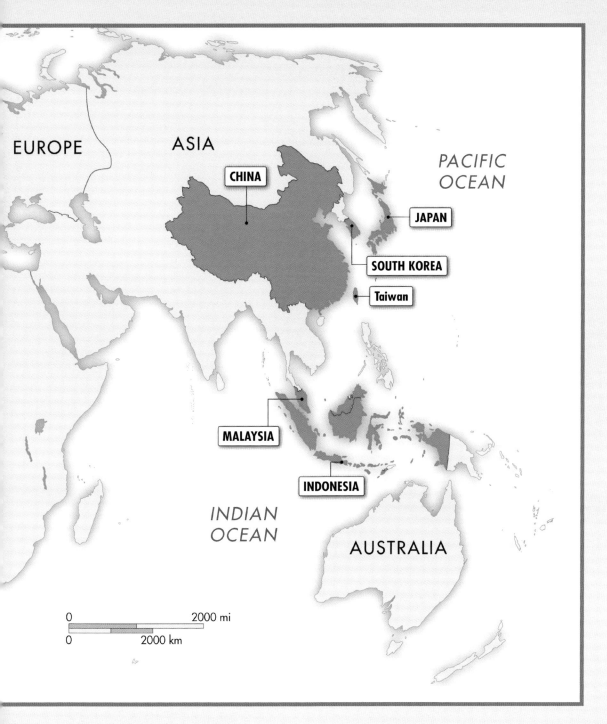

EUROPE

ASIA

PACIFIC OCEAN

CHINA

JAPAN

SOUTH KOREA

Taiwan

MALAYSIA

INDONESIA

INDIAN OCEAN

AUSTRALIA

0   2000 mi

0   2000 km

lives naturally and where it has invaded.

GLOSSARY

amphibians (am-FIB-ee-uhnz) cold-blooded animals that live some part of their life in or near water, and some part of their life on land

chorus (KOR-uhss) a group of individuals singing together, sometimes used to describe a group of frogs croaking

chytrid fungus (KY-trid FUHN-guhss) an organism that produces spores, is related to molds, and causes amphibians to become ill and die

collagen (KOL-uh-jen) a substance in animal bodies that helps to hold cells and tissues together

continent (KON-tuh-nuhnt) one of Earth's major landmasses

environments (en-VYE-ruhn-muhnts) all of the natural surroundings where plants and animals live, including the weather, water, and food sources

eradicate (i-RAD-uh-kate) to completely wipe something out

habitat (HAB-uh-tat) the place where an animal or plant naturally lives and grows

hatcheries (HATCH-er-eez) places where young animals such as fish or chickens are hatched from eggs and briefly cared for

hibernate (HYE-bur-nate) to spend the winter in a safe location, with greatly slowed bodily activities

metamorphosis (met-uh-MOR-fuh-siss) a complete change in body form

organism (OR-guh-niz-uhm) living thing

poaching (POHCH-ing) illegal hunting

predators (PRED-uh-turz) animals that hunt and eat other animals

prey (PRAY) animals that are hunted and eaten by other animals

resorbed (ree-ZORBD) taken back into the body to be used again

FOR MORE INFORMATION

Books

Buller, Laura, and Barry Clarke. *Amphibian*. New York: DK Children, 2005.

Moffett, Mark. *Face to Face with Frogs*. Washington, DC:
National Geographic Children's Books, 2008.

Web Sites

Animal Diversity Web
animaldiversity.ummz.umich.edu/site/accounts/information/Rana_catesbeiana.html
Information about the biology of bullfrogs

National Geographic Kids—American Bullfrogs
kids.nationalgeographic.com/Animals/CreatureFeature/American-bullfrog
A Web site with information and images of bullfrogs

INDEX

ABOUT THE AUTHOR

Susan H. Gray has a master's degree in zoology. She has written more than 90 science and reference books for children, and especially loves writing about animals. Susan also likes to garden and play the piano. She lives in Cabot, Arkansas, with her husband Michael and many pets.

Amira

ZAHARA

NADEZHDA

YUME

T.S.

MAY – – 2023

NAMING CEREMONY

written by Seina Wedlick | illustrated by Jenin Mohammed

Abrams Books for Young Readers
New York

Amira is excited.

Today is her baby sister's naming ceremony.

Mama puts a coral bracelet on baby sister's wrist.

"How do I pick a name for baby sister?" Amira asks.

"Think of something meaningful that you would want her to have. A blessing, a wish, a story. Each of your names were carefully picked, just for you," says Mama.

"Now, baby sister will also get her own special names," says Amira.

"Yes, just as special as that little dimple in your cheek."

Amira sits quietly for a minute.

"What name do you have for baby sister?" she asks.

"You'll have to wait and see," says Mama. "We will start as soon as the baby wakes up."

"When you wake up, little one, I will have the perfect gift for you," Amira whispers.

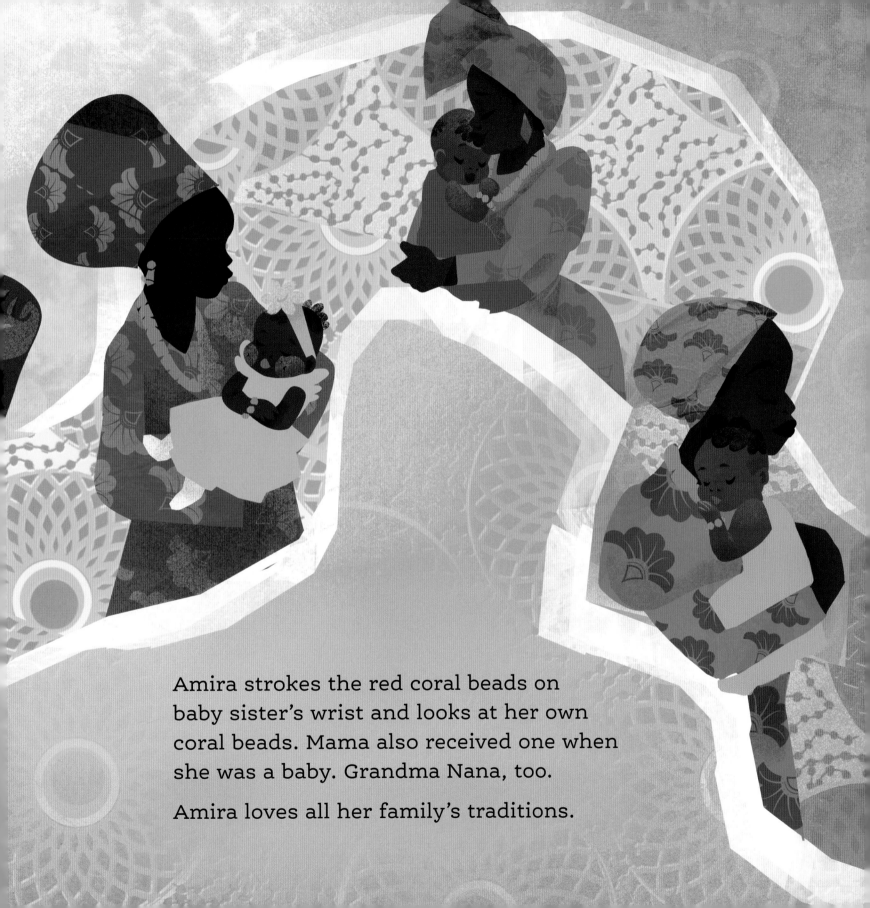

Amira strokes the red coral beads on baby sister's wrist and looks at her own coral beads. Mama also received one when she was a baby. Grandma Nana, too.

Amira loves all her family's traditions.

Ding!
Dong!

Guests!

It is Grandma Nana
with the cousins!

The little twins,
Onize and Oricha,
run past Amira,
laughing and giggling.

Mmm hmm. Amira takes a whiff of the tray of akara.

"What gift do you have for baby sister?"
asks Amira with a mouthful of fried beancake.

"**Shakira**," says Grandma Nana.

Shakira! Surely, baby sister has a lot
to be thankful for.

But what if baby sister doesn't like the name she picks?

Ding!
Dong!

Amira jumps up and
rushes to the front door.

It is Miki.

"Hi Amira!"

"What gift do you have
for baby sister?" asks Amira.

"*Akahana*.
This means *bright red flower*.
I picked this for your baby sister
from our garden."

Red flower! What a beautiful name.
Surely, baby sister will be just as lovely.

Ding!

Dong!

It is Uncle Ali,
the storyteller.

Boom
 Boom
  Boom!

He plays Amira's favorite tune.

She starts to dance and asks, "Uncle Ali, what gift do you have for baby sister?"

"**Uhwe**," he says with a wink.

Uhwe. Moonlight. Everyone knows stories are best told at night. Surely, baby sister will be a wonderful storyteller like Uncle.

Rat
Tat
Tat.

Uncle Ali plays another tune on his drum.

Soon Onize and Oricha are dancing along to his stories.

Ding!
Dong!

It is her best friend.

"Hi Amira!" says Tamas.

"What gift do you have for baby sister?" asks Amira.

"**Rubik**. I will teach her how to solve it."

Rubik! Surely, baby sister will be very brilliant.

Shakira.

Akahana.

Uhwe.

Rubik.

Such interesting names.
Amira wonders if she should change her gift.

Will baby sister like the name she picks?

But it is too late to change her gift now because baby sister is awake!

"Baby sister, I have a present for you. I'll be right back."

Amira hurries to the garden and announces loudly:

"Baby sister is awake! It is time to start!"

She runs to the kitchen.

"Baby sister is awake! It is time to give her gifts!"

She stops by the playroom.

"Baby sister is AWAKE!"

Amira hurries back. She does not want to
be late for baby sister's naming ceremony.

The kitchen is empty.

The garden is empty.

There is no one at the front door.

Everyone is squashed in the living room.

It is tight and cozy.

"Thank you all for gathering with us today.
We are honored that you have chosen
to come and celebrate with us," says Papa.

"The name we have chosen is . . ."

The room is silent.

"**Habiba**," says Mama.

"Habiba means *beloved*. And today, we give Habiba the gift of names."

Amira looks at the room filled with family and friends
from all over the world. Beloved. It is perfect for baby sister.

And so, it begins. Everyone names Habiba until it is Amira's turn.

Baby sister stares at Amira expectantly.

Amira twiddles her fingers together. Hers is the last gift.

She takes a deep breath.

"I name her **Otta**. This means friend."

"You will always have me as your friend,"
Amira whispers to Habiba.

Baby sister smiles her special smile,
with a little dimple in her cheek.

"I love you, Otta."

Naming Ceremony Tradition

In West Africa, there is a tradition that shortly after a baby is born, family and friends come together to give the baby names whose meanings are considered blessings. This is a happy occasion at the start of a new life that forms a bond between the name-giver and the recipient. A big part of naming ceremonies is opening it up to more than just the nuclear family and giving extended family and friends a chance to be part of the joy of welcoming a new life.

Oftentimes, the name-giver will call the baby the name they gave them when they were born, or they can decide to call the child the name the parents have chosen. It varies a lot.

In some cultures, names are generally given by the elders in the family. Extended family and friends can give a name in addition to a small monetary gift. The family of the child will usually have a feast prepared to celebrate with their guests.

Many countries around the world have similar naming traditions. The names of babies are sometimes picked based on their religion or culture. Some babies are named after relatives or based on their birth order, the circumstances of their birth, or the name-giver's hopes and wishes for the baby.

For my children, whose names were written on my heart long before they were born.
—SW

To my big sister, Ansaria. If I attended your naming ceremony, I would give you a name that meant *intelligence*.
—JM

The art in this book was made with digital and mixed media.

Cataloging-in-Publication Data has been applied for and may be obtained from the Library of Congress.

ISBN 978-1-4197-5626-9

Text © 2023 Seina Wedlick

Illustrations © 2023 Jenin Mohammed

Book design by Jade Rector and Natalie Padberg Bartoo

Published in 2023 by Abrams Books for Young Readers, an imprint of ABRAMS.

Printed and bound in China

10 9 8 7 6 5 4 3 2 1

Abrams Books for Young Readers are available at special discounts when purchased in quantity for premiums and promotions as well as fundraising or educational use. Special editions can also be created to specification. For details, contact specialsales@abramsbooks.com or the address below.

Abrams® is a registered trademark of Harry N. Abrams, Inc.

ABRAMS The Art of Books
195 Broadway, New York, NY 10007
abramsbooks.com

UHWE

SHAKI

Habiba